Swimsuit from a
publicity still

Pretty Ladies
(MGM, 1925)
[In this film, still called Lucille Le Sueur]

Plate 1

Sally, Irene and Mary
(MGM, 1925)

Our Dancing Daughters
(MGM, 1928)
Costume: David Cox

Plate 2

Our Blushing Brides
(MGM, 1930)
Costume: Adrian

Possessed
(MGM, 1931)

Plate 3

Do Not Cut Out White Area Between Arm and Body

Grand Hotel
(MGM, 1932)
Costume: Adrian

Rain
(United Artists, 1932)

Plate 4

Letty Lynton
(MGM, 1932)
Costume: Adrian

Plate 5

Two costumes from
Dancing Lady
(MGM, 1933)
Costumes: Adrian

Plate 6

Sadie McKee
(MGM, 1934)
Costume: Adrian

I Live My Life
(MGM, 1935)
Costume: Adrian

Plate 7

The Gorgeous Hussy
(MGM, 1936)
Costume: Adrian

The Bride Wore Red
(MGM, 1937)
Costume: Adrian

Plate 8

The Last of Mrs. Cheyney
(MGM, 1937)
Costume: Adrian

Mannequin
(MGM, 1938)
Costume: Adrian

Plate 9

Ice Follies of 1939
(MGM, 1939)
Costume: Adrian

The Women
(MGM, 1939)
Costume: Adrian

Plate 10

Susan and God
(MGM, 1940)
Costume: Adrian

When Ladies Meet
(MGM, 1941)
Costume: Adrian

Plate 11

Two costumes from
Mildred Pierce
(Warner Bros., 1945)
Costumes: Milo Anderson

Plate 12

Humoresque
(Warner Bros., 1946)
Costume: Adrian

Flamingo Road
(Warner Bros., 1949)
Costume: William Travilla

Plate 13

Harriet Craig
(Columbia, 1950)
Costume: Sheila O'Brien

Torch Song
(MGM, 1953)
Costume: Helen Rose

Plate 14

Johnny Guitar
(Republic, 1954)
Costume: Sheila O'Brien

Female on the Beach
(Universal, 1955)
Costume: Sheila O'Brien

Do Not Cut Out White Areas Between Arm and Sash and Between Sash and Body

Plate 15

I Saw What You Did
(Universal, 1965)

Berserk!
(Columbia, 1967)

Plate 16